THE ROLE OF WOMEN IN THE AMERICAN REVOLUTION

History Picture Books
Children's History Books

BABY PROFESSOR
EDUCATION KIDS

Speedy Publishing LLC

40 E. Main St. #1156

Newark, DE 19711

www.speedypublishing.com

Copyright 2017

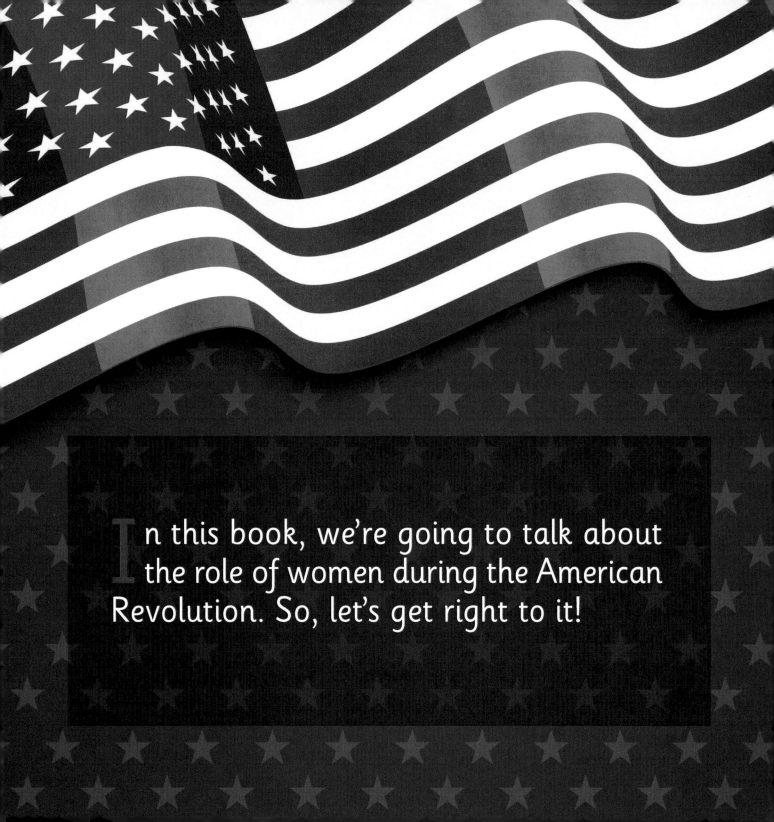

In this book, we're going to talk about the role of women during the American Revolution. So, let's get right to it!

Battle of New Orleans
(American Revolutionary War)

During the American Revolutionary War, women took on some traditional roles as well as some very unconventional roles. Women did their part to help the country gain independence from Britain.

Traditional roles included seamstresses to create uniforms and flags, cooks to prepare meals for the soldiers, maids to take care of the work in living quarters, and, eventually, nurses to care for the sick and dying. Many women didn't travel but instead took care of their homes or farms.

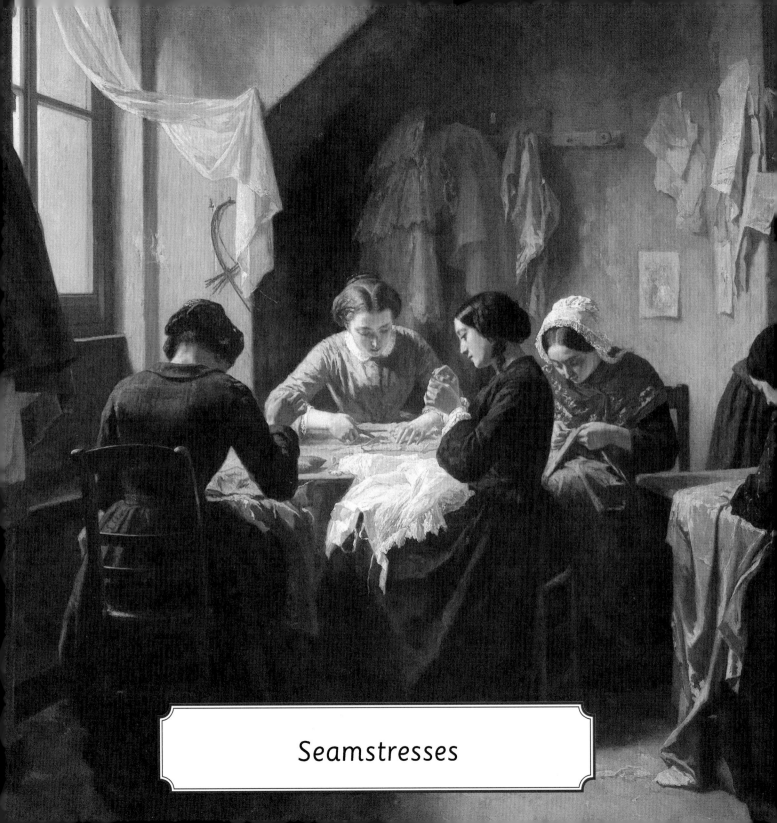

Seamstresses

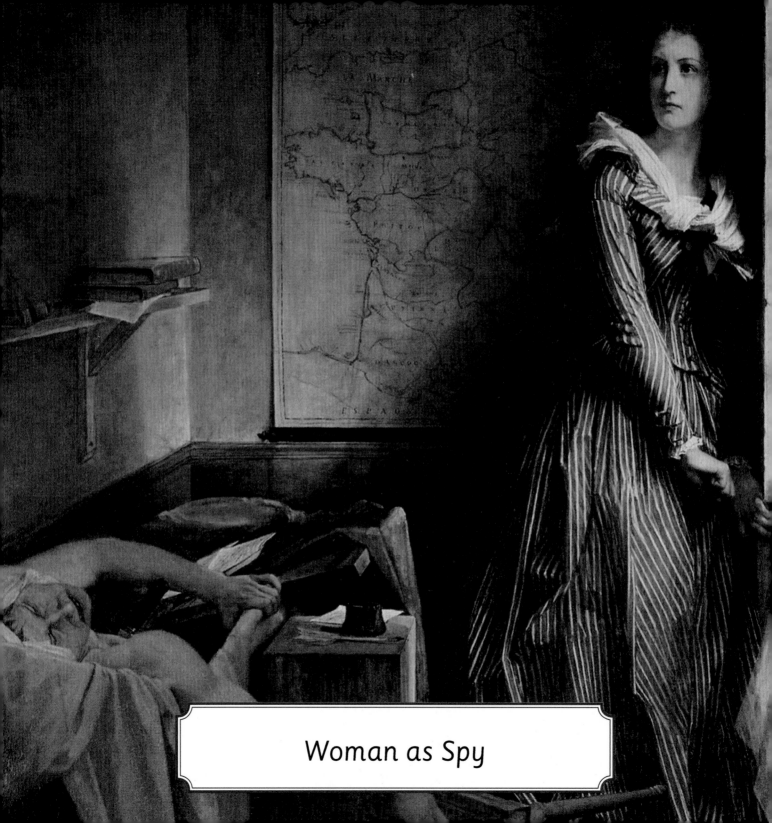

Woman as Spy

Since their men were gone, their responsibilities increased and they stepped up to perform these duties.

Unconventional roles included participating as soldiers and sometimes even as secret spies!

WHO WERE THE CAMP FOLLOWERS?

Sometimes the mothers of soldiers or their wives or daughters followed the army to their camps. They needed protection and food because they had no means to make a living after the men joined the war effort. These camp followers were asked to take on jobs once the army got organized. It soon became clear that their efforts would be useful and would free up the men for the business of fighting.

Molly Pitcher fighting in the war

COOKS, MAIDS AND SEAMSTRESSES

Men usually fulfilled the support roles in the army in those days. Male soldiers were assigned duties to cook, clean, do the laundry, or sew. Soon, every male soldier was needed in the fight, so it was natural that the camp followers would be enlisted to take over these duties. Many of these women were impoverished and welcomed the chance to do an extension of the housework they did in their homes in exchange for food and protection.

Margaret Corbin from Philadelphia was a camp follower who became famous for her bravery. Margaret had traveled with her husband when he joined the artillery in Pennsylvania. He had a specialized job as a matross, which is someone who provides the ammunition for, as well as fires, cannons.

Margaret Corbin

View of the Attack Against Fort Washington

In 1776, at the Battle of Fort Washington, he was killed during battle leaving his post at the cannon. Margaret was with him and continued to fire the cannon until she was struck by enemy fire. Unfortunately, the colonists didn't win that battle. She was taken as a prisoner by the British but later released. A pension was given to her for her bravery in service of the war effort.

NURSES

In the early days of the war, nurses had not been on staff. However, in 1777, George Washington requested that his officers go to the camp followers to request that they come on board as nurses. They would be paid 24 cents daily plus a food ration.

War Nurses

A Matron

There would be one supervisory nurse, who was called a matron, and ten other nurses for every hundred of the men who were wounded or sick. The supervisory nurses received about 50 cents plus the ration, every day.

Physicians performed the surgeries and other medical tasks, but the support of the women nurses was critical. They fed the patients and bathed them. They scrubbed the hospital rooms and emptied and cleaned the chamber pots, which were used by the soldiers to go to the bathroom. They were sometimes asked to do cooking as well.

Go Chair

The nurses came up with interesting ways to keep the soldiers comfortable as they healed from their wounds. They created a type of wheelchair called a "go-chair." They also had these chairs with fans to cool the soldiers.

They used stone bottles to create "hot-water bottles" for their beds. To make their diet palatable, they created a special porridge from milk and oatmeal. They added butter, a few eggs, and orange extract to give it flavor and they also made a type of tea out of beef juice.

Oatmeal Porridge

Battle of Trenton

Even though the pay was good, many women didn't want to become nurses because so many soldiers died and also because many of the caregivers got sick and died as well because they contracted diseases from the sick soldiers.

March to Valley Forge

Two gallant nurses were Mary Waters who came to Philadelphia from Dublin in 1766 and worked as a nurse in the army.

In 1777, another notable nurse, Mary Pricely,
served on a ship called the Defense.

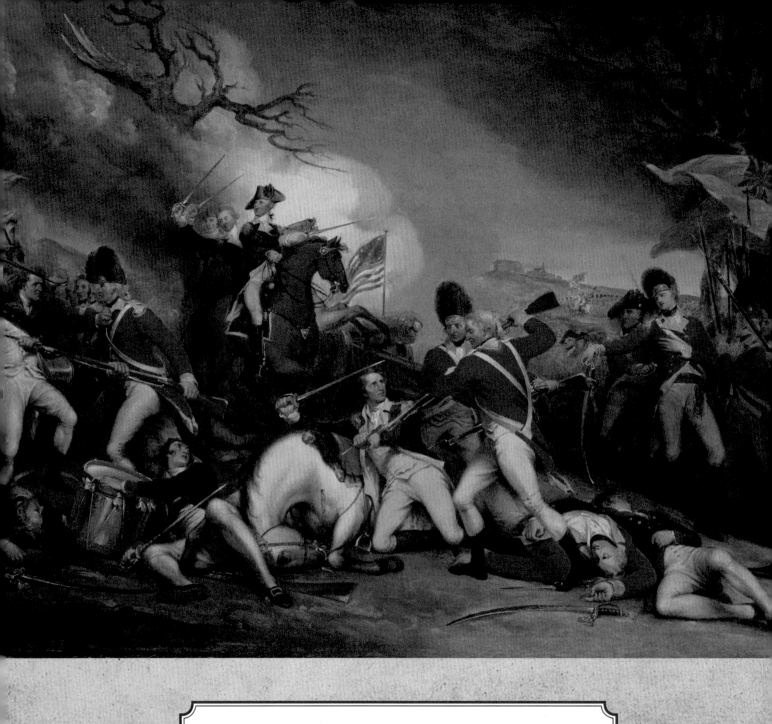

Battle of Princeton

SECRET SOLDIERS

Women were forbidden from joining the military, but some wanted to fight. In order to get away with it, they sheared off their hair, bound their chests, and gave themselves men's names. Most of these women were impoverished and they joined to make money, but they also wanted to help in the fight for independence.

The Revolutionary War started in the colony of Massachusetts. A majority of the women were from that area. In 1781, a young woman by the name of Deborah Sampson changed her name to Robert Shurtliff and was a soldier for a year before her true identity was discovered.

Deborah Sampson

Paul Revere

S he was still promised a pension for her service. However, when the war was over, she had a hard time getting the money, so she worked with a writer to put together a biography. She went out on a tour and dressed in military uniform while she was lecturing and telling the story of her war experiences. She even performed maneuvers with firearms to prove that she had been a soldier. The famous Patriot Paul Revere fought to get her pension for her after the war.

Another woman soldier was Nancy Bailey. She joined in 1777 under the false name Sam Gay. She was promoted to the position of Corporal before her true identity was discovered. She was arrested and thrown in prison. When she got out, she joined again and served for several weeks before she was unmasked again!

Nancy was thrown in prison

American Maid

SECRET SPIES

As women went about as cooks, maids, and seamstresses, they heard the men talking about military campaigns. Some of these women were working in the British camps, but their loyalties were with the Patriots and they wanted American Independence.

They paid attention to what the British were saying about troop movements as well as their strategies and plans. They took mental notes and then later reported what they heard to the Patriots.

The war was fought in their neighborhoods and communities so it was easy for them to travel to houses nearby to relay the news without being caught by the British.

Battle of Bunker Hill

Siege of Boston Artillery

During the Siege of Boston, there wasn't a centralized spy ring, but when the war was centered in New York, the army established a spy ring, called the Culper Spy Ring. They even had a code number, which was 355, especially for women operatives working in the ring.

One famous spy was a woman by the name of Hannah Blair from North Carolina. She owned a farm where she would shelter Patriots. She took care of soldiers who were hiding from the British or Loyalists. She fed them, got them medical assistance, and gave them messages to pass to their commanders. When nearby Loyalists found out about her, they set her farm ablaze and it burned down. After the war, Congress issued her a pension for her brave service.

Hannah Blair On Her Farm

Martha Washington

OTHER NOTABLE WOMEN OF THE AMERICAN REVOLUTION

MARTHA WASHINGTON

Martha was George Washington's wife. She provided emotional support during the battles. At Valley Forge she stayed with George and provided comforting words to the wounded soldiers to keep their spirits up. She was there during their winter encampments for eight long years during the war.

ABIGAIL ADAMS

During the war, Abigail Adams advised her husband John Adams and kept his morale up by writing him letters in the thousands. Her husband became a Founding Father and the second President of the United States.

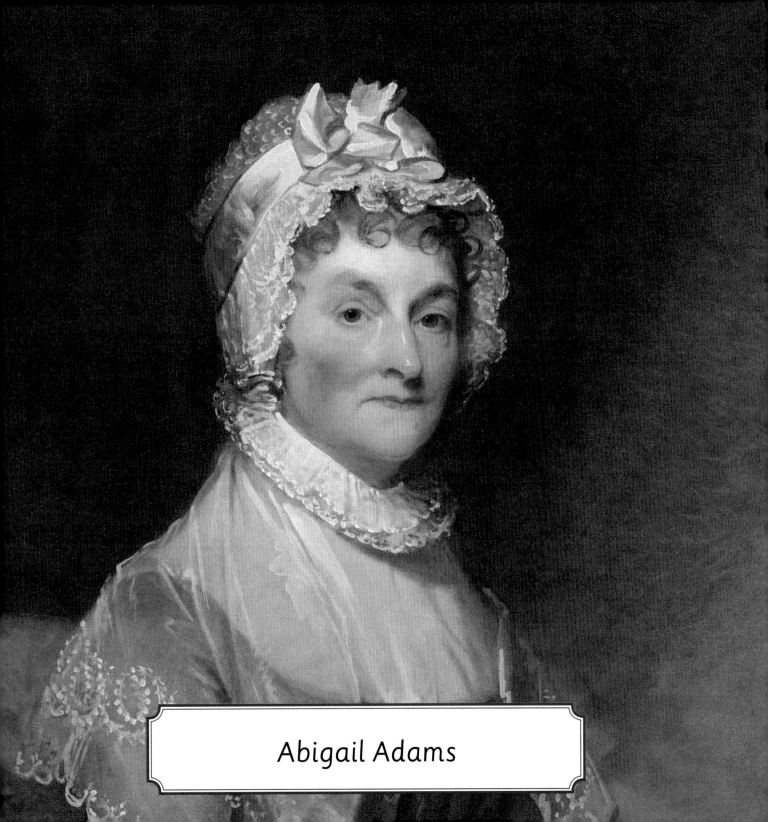

Abigail Adams

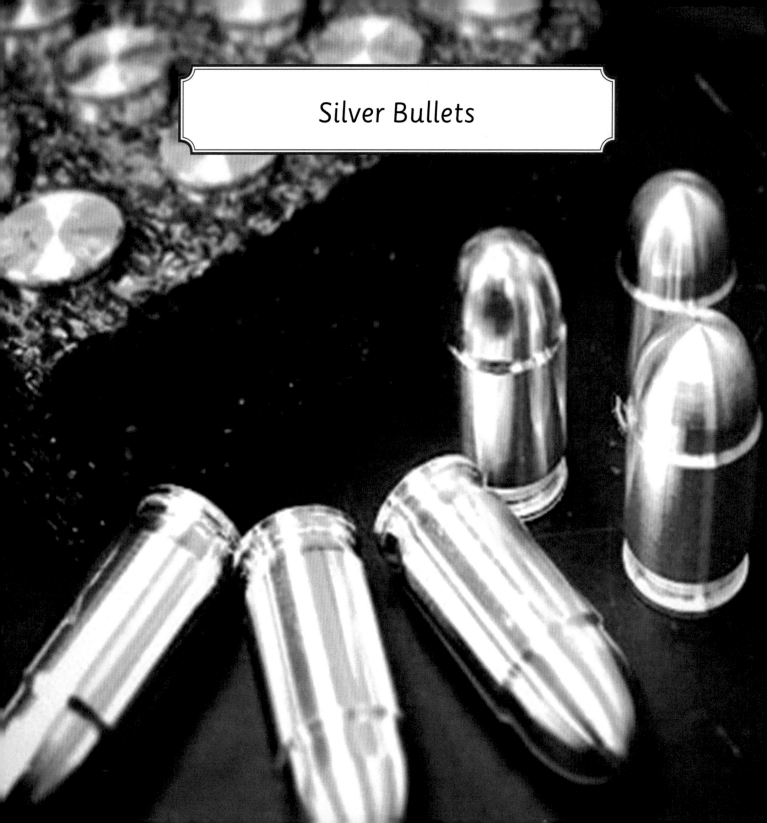

Silver Bullets

Their home was close to the fighting and upon hearing that the soldiers had no ammunition for their muskets, she had silver and steel from her own property melted down to make ammunition for them. Seeing her sacrifice helped the troops regain their morale during the difficult fight.

KATE BARRY

Just as Paul Revere had done, Kate Barry rode on horseback to warn the soldiers of the Continental Army that the British were on their way. This warning assisted the colonists in succeeding against the British in the Battle of Cowpens.

Battle of Cowpens

Nancy Hart Holding Off Loyalists

NANCY HART

A loyal Patriot, Nancy was a spy for the revolutionary cause. She wandered into the Loyalists camps dressed as a very simpleminded man so she could gather intelligence to send back to the Patriots. She held off a number of Loyalists by shooting two of them to delay them until help arrived at her home.

MERCY OTIS WARREN

A prominent writer, Mercy worked to help make the colonists' beliefs widely known. She acted as a consultant to important leaders of the new nation.

Mercy Otis Warren

Awesome! Now you know more about the amazing contributions women made during the American Revolution. You can find more History books from Baby Professor by searching the website of your favorite book retailer.

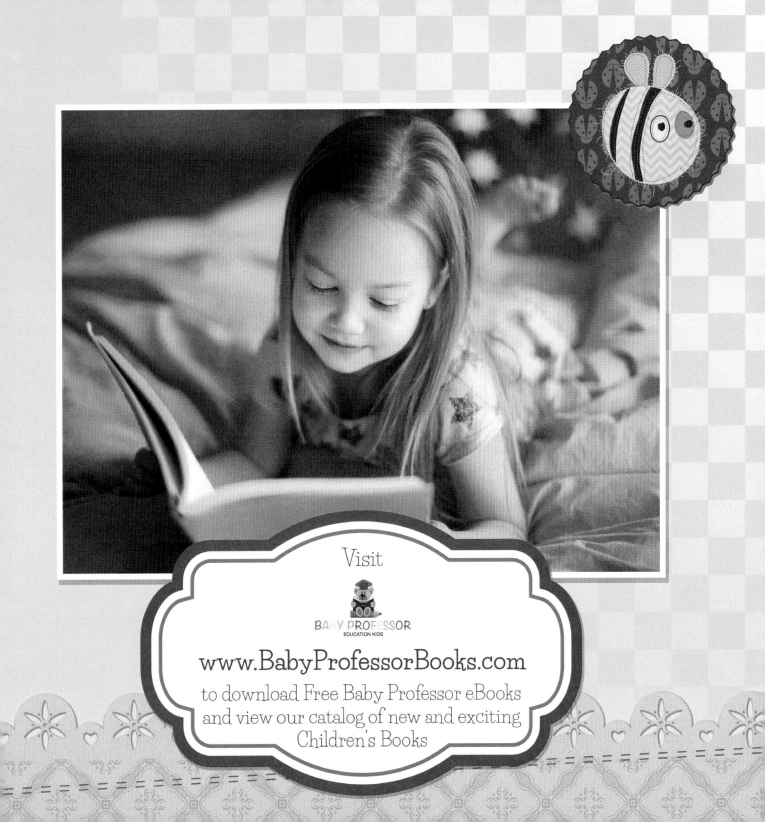

Made in the USA
Middletown, DE
08 January 2019